FIGURE SKATING

A TRUE BOOK

by

Larry Dane Brimner

Children's Press®
A Division of Grolier Publishing

New York London Hong Kong Sydney
Danbury, Connecticut

U.S. figure skater
Nancy Kerrigan

Reading Consultant
Linda Cornwell
Learning Resource Consultant
Indiana Department
of Education

Author's Dedication:
For Lee Bennett Hopkins

Library of Congress Cataloging-in-Publication Data

Brimner, Larry Dane
    Figure Skating / by Larry Dane Brimner.
        p.   cm. — (A true book)
    Includes bibliographical references (p.) and index.
    Summary: Sketches the history of ice skating from its beginning as a means of travel to its current status as a sport; discusses the contributions of Sonja Henie and other Olympic Stars.
    ISBN 0-516-20440-8 (lib. bdg.)   0-516-26204-1 (pbk.)
    1. Skating—History—Juvenile literature. 2. Skaters—Biography—Juvenile literature. [1. Ice skating. 2. Ice skaters.] I. Title. II. Series.
GV850.4.B75 1997
796.91'2—dc21   97-9014
                                                                                                        CIP
                                                                                                        AC

Contents

Sonja Henie's skating style shocked the judges at the 1924 Winter Olympics.

A Legend

At the first Olympic Winter Games in 1924, an eleven-year-old figure skater took the ice. Her name was Sonja Henie. At the time, women skaters wore black, ankle-length skirts. They skated dull programs.

Sonja, however, was not boring. Coached by her father,

she had more flash and style than most other skaters. She wore a short, white satin dress. Fur trimmed her shoulders. When Sonja skated, she combined ballet and athletic ability. Her routine shocked the judges. They didn't just react to her short costume. Sonja dared to jump—and jumping was reserved for men. The judges thought it was not a proper activity for a lady. Sonja finished the 1924 Winter Games in last place.

Sonja's skating program included daring leaps and spins.

True Olympians, however, don't give up. Sonja kept skating. Over the next four years, the girl from Oslo, Norway, continued to dance on ice.

She continued to jump and spin. In 1927, Sonja won her first World Championship. The very next year, she competed at the 1928 Olympic Winter Games. This time, fifteen-year-old Sonja won the gold medal in figure skating. She would go on to win two more gold medals at the 1932 and 1936 Games.

Sonja's story did not end there. In the 1930s, Olympic skaters did not become professionals. There were no ice-skating shows. Sonja changed all that. After the 1936 Games, she decided to tour with her own ice show. It was a hit! And it made Sonja famous around the world.

After her Olympic career ended, Sonja brought her dazzling skating talent to Hollywood. One of Sonja's ice-skating characters was Alice in *Alice in Wonderland*.

Following the ice show, she turned her attention to Hollywood and making movies. By 1939, Sonja was making more money than any other woman in the world. She was a legend. And she inspired countless young people to take up the sport of figure skating.

The Early Years

Nobody knows exactly when people began to skate on ice. It is clear, however, that the first ice skaters didn't skate for recreation and fun. They skated because they had to. In cold northern lands, skating was a quick and easy way to get from place to place. It was a way to escape

In this Dutch village (above), the people skated both for work and for fun. Skating provided an easy way to travel during the winter (left).

attacking enemies. It was a way to hunt for food during long winters.

The first skates were made of animal bones. The bones were tied to shoes with leather straps. Skates were also made of wood.

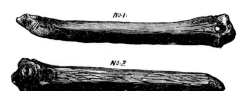

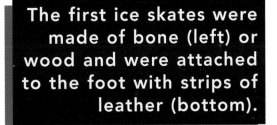

The first ice skates were made of bone (left) or wood and were attached to the foot with strips of leather (bottom).

Dutch Wooden Skate

Eventually, the people of Holland made skates with iron and, later, steel blades. Skating became a part of daily life, and interest in it spread far beyond Holland's shores.

Skating became popular in the United States in the nineteenth century. In this photograph, people enjoy skating in Central Park, New York City.

ANCIENT SKATE. GERMAN SKATE THE SKATE OF THE POOR. DUTCH SKATE. RUSSIAN SKATE AMERICAN SKATE

Skates from around the world

The biggest problem with the early skates was finding a good way to attach the blades to the skater's feet. Leather straps were used, but they quickly wore out. This problem was finally solved around 1800. Blades were permanently attached to boots for the first time, and little has changed since then.

Skating Becomes a Sport

In Holland, skating was mainly a way to travel long distances. But in the 1700s, the British developed the fluted skate, and things changed. Fluted skates had a groove down the center of the blade. This made turning easier, and

Fluted skates allow modern figure skaters to turn quickly.

soon people began skating for fun. Fluted skates are still used by today's figure skaters.

How did figure skating get its name? Once skaters began skating on fluted skates, they began carving patterns in the

ice. The patterns, called "figures," were etched in the ice.
They remained there even
after the skater left. The first
figure skaters didn't dance on
ice. They didn't jump or spin.

Figure skating was
originally concerned
with carving patterns
in the ice. Today,
figure skaters are
more concerned with
graceful movement.

Since 1992, skaters have gained more freedom to add their own moves to performances— such as this flip!

They drew patterns (or "figures") with their skates, so they were called "figure skaters."

Before 1992, every Olympic figure skater had to trace set patterns on the ice. This event, called "compulsory figures," is no longer required in Olympic competition.

The Olympic Events

Today, figure skating is both a sport and an art. It is a combination of dance, fluid movement, and athletic ability. At competitions, several judges carefully watch each skater's routine. Each judge awards a skater's performance two marks between zero and six.

U.S. figure skater Michelle Kwan's performances are full of graceful and athletic movements (left). The judges' scores are posted on a scoreboard (above).

The first score is for technical ability. The second score is for artistic impression. Skaters may compete in three events: individual skating, pair skat-ing, and ice dancing.

According to current rules, individual skaters perform twice during a competition. The first performance is a two-minute forty-second (short) program with eight required moves, or "elements." The second performance is a freestyle (long) program. The long program gives the skater more time and freedom for artistic expression. The skater with the highest combined score wins the competition.

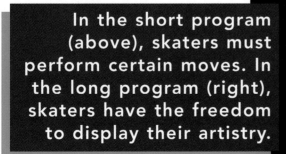

In the short program (above), skaters must perform certain moves. In the long program (right), skaters have the freedom to display their artistry.

In pair skating, a man and a woman skate together. Scoring is similar to that for individual skating. The technical program requires each pair to perform elements. One of the required elements, the death spiral, originated in the early 1900s. To perform the death spiral, the man holds the woman by the legs. He spins her around in a circle so that her head nearly scrapes the ice.

Pair skaters must work as a team. They must perform

In pair skating, the skaters must perform a move called the death spiral (top right). Pair skaters must perform difficult moves at the same time (left).

jumps and spins perfectly. Judges carefully watch each pair for smoothness and exact timing. A couple whose individual movements are mirror images of each other will receive high marks.

Ice dancers must keep contact with each other.

Ice dancing is a fairly recent Olympic event. It has been part of the Olympic Winter Games since 1976. What makes ice dancing different from pair skating is that dancers may not use lifts and throws. They may separate only briefly. Also, they must skate as one intertwined unit. They perform traditional dance steps on ice, but they must also show originality.

Precision Skating

The latest type of ice skating is called "precision." It began in Ann Arbor, Michigan, when teenagers performed a routine that resembled the Rockettes of Radio City Music Hall. They called themselves "the Hockettes."

Today, the sport is growing popular. Teams of eight to thirty-two skaters perform precision routines, skating in unison to music. Precision skating is not an Olympic sport, but someday it might be.

Stars on Ice

Figure skating is sometimes called the "Jewel of the Winter Olympics." This is because it is a graceful and beautiful sport. Also, people enjoy watching it on television. People may not know Alberto Tomba, the Olympic skier. However, just about

Skaters who perform in the Olympics become known around the world.

everyone knows figure skater Oksana Baiul, and that she won a gold medal in 1994. This is because figure skaters are the stars of the Olympics— they're stars on ice.

Oksana Baiul was only sixteen when she won the Olympic gold medal for the Ukraine at Lillehammer in 1994. People were surprised. The day before she won the medal, she had collided with another skater. She suffered a back injury and required three stitches to close a gash in her leg. Her pain was so great that the International Olympic Committee gave her permission to take pain killers. But

Oksana Baiul's grace and style won her an Olympic gold medal.

Oksana had faced obstacles before in her short life. Her father deserted the family when she was two. Her mother died when she was thirteen. A wrenched back and pain killers were minor obstacles by comparison. They didn't stop her from giving the performance of a lifetime.

Baiul reacts to the news that she has won the gold medal.

Elvis Stojko is known for his unique style.

Elvis Stojko won a second-place silver medal for Canada at the 1994 Winter Games. His skating style is uniquely his own. With a black belt in karate, he often adds kung fu

Stojko performs
a difficult jump.

moves to his routines. His performances are energetic, athletic,
and artistic. He loves jumping so
much that some call him "Air
Stojko." Elvis, who was named
after Elvis Presley, won the World
Championships in 1994 and 1995.
Look for him at the 1998 Olympic
Winter Games in Japan.

Sergei Grinkov and Ekaterina Gordeeva finish a program.

Ekaterina Gordeeva and Sergei Grinkov were Olympic gold medalists for pair skating in both 1988 and 1994. People gave them a nickname, "the gorilla and the flea," because Sergei was eleven inches taller than Katya. Even so, when they skated, this husband and wife matched each other stride for stride, jump for jump, spin for spin. Tragically, Sergei died suddenly of a heart attack in 1995.

Grinkov prepares to catch Gordeeva.

Jayne Torvill and Christopher Dean always enjoy themselves while skating

Jayne Torvill and Christopher Dean are Great Britain's legendary ice dancing team. They are considered the greatest ice dancers in the history of the sport. But they didn't start out great. In fact, they finished fifth at the 1980 Olympic Winter Games. After that, though, they went on to win three World Championships. When it was time for the 1984 Olympic Winter Games, Jayne and Christopher were ready. It was Valentine's Day, and the two skated to Ravel's *Bolero*, a love story with a sad ending. When the scores were flashed, they received a perfect 6.0 from

Even when performing difficult maneuvers, Torvill and Dean must maintain contact.

all nine judges. It was no sad ending for this pair. Their fame is so great today that they are known simply as Torvill and Dean.

What makes Olympic skaters different from other figure skaters is their desire for perfection. Some Olympians achieve a gold, silver, or bronze medal. Others do not. But even if they do not win a medal, all Olympians are winners because they are not satisfied with "good enough." They are always pushing themselves to greater heights.

Olympic skaters constantly push themselves to a higher level of performance.

To Find Out More

Here are some additional resources to help you learn more about skating:

 **Books**

Brimner, Larry Dane. **Speed Skating.** Children's Press, 1997.

Brimner, Larry Dane. **The Winter Olympics.** Children's Press, 1997.

Greenspan, Bud. **100 Greatest Moments in Olympic History.** General Publishing Group, 1995.

Gutman, Dan. **Ice Skating: From Axels to Zambonis©.** Viking Books, 1995.

Malley, Stephen. **A Kid's Guide to the Nineteen Ninety-Four Winter Olympics.** Bantam Press, 1994.

Wallechinsky, David. **The Complete Book of the Winter Olympics.** Little, Brown & Co., 1993.

44

Organizations and Online Sites

United States Figure Skating Association

20 First Street
Colorado Springs, CO 80906
http://members.gnn.com/ USFSA/index.htm

An extensive list of figure skating clubs throughout the United States.

2002 Winter Olympic Games Home Page

http://www.SLC2002.org

A growing web page that provides information on the 2002 Winter Olympics in Salt Lake City.

Canadian Figure Skating Association

http://www.cfsa.ca/

A central site providing facts and sources about Canadian skating clubs.

Official 1998 Olympic Web Site

http://www.nagano. olympic.org

A great source of information on the events of the 1998 Winter Olympics.

Winter Sports Page

http://www.wintersports.org

A central site to explore winter sports and links to other sites.

Important Words

artistic impression score given to a skater for the overall presentation of a program

elements moves that every skater must perform

fluted skate skate blade with a groove down the center, allowing easy turns

long program performance in which skaters are free to show their artistic ability

short program performance in which the skater must complete certain moves

technical ability score that reflects a skater's skill at performing required moves

Index

Meet the Author

Larry Dane Brimner is the author of several books for Children's Press, including five True Books on the Winter Olympics. He is a member of the Authors Guild and the Society of Children's Book Writers and Illustrators. Mr. Brimner makes his home in Southern California and the Rocky Mountains.